Uncle Bob's Red Flannel Bible Camp

(From Eden to the Ark)

BY

STEVE VERNON

STARK RAVEN PRESS

2014

Have you EVER sat down and tried to actually READ the Holy Bible? All of those thou-shalt-nots and yea-verilies and don't you DARE get me started on all of that begatting business!

That all changed the day that Uncle Bob caught me trying to skip out on Sunday School. He sat me down and he told me the whole entire story - from Eden to the Ark - in a way that made total perfect sense to me. Uncle Bob taught me that the Bible was filled with action and heroes and adventure and a WHOLE lot of straight out funny.

If you have faith - well, you ought to sit down and listen to my Uncle Bob.

If you have begun to DOUBT your faith - well, you ought to sit down and give a listen to my Uncle Bob too.

If you don't think that God doesn't have himself a high old sense of humor - well you REALLY ought to sit down and listen to my Uncle Bob.

In fact, everybody in the world NEEDS an Uncle Bob.

You do too - whether you know it or not.

Uncle Bob's Red Flannel Bible Camp - From Eden To The Ark is a short, fast FUN retelling of the first few stories of the Holy Bible. It will SHOCK you if you don't have much of a sense of humor. It will tickle you silly if your giggle bone isn't broke.

UNCLE BOB'S RED FLANNEL BIBLE CAMP

By Steve Vernon

Cover Art: Keri Knutson

ISBN-13: 978-1-927765-21-0

First Edition – March 2, 2014

Dedication

To the Reverend Dale Allison

of the Capreol United Church

(Northern Ontario – God's country)

Who played football with the kids after service

and

to

my

Grandmother

who made me go to church every Sunday whether I liked it or not.

Introduction

NEARLY EVERYONE IN THE WHOLE WIDE WORLD needs an Uncle Bob.

Mind you, my Uncle Bob isn't all that much to look at.

As near as I can tell he is ALWAYS dressed in red flannel. His shirt looks like he might have picked it up at Wal-Mart about three days following the first Mesopotamian War. My Uncle Bob is just a little teapot of a man with a sort of a question mark slump in his shoulders, a breath that smells a little of tobacco and Listerine, and a belly-bulge that looks as if a medicine ball had given birth to quadrupal-quintuplets inside of his stomach

Uncle Bob is a straight talker – which means that he ALWAYS says just exactly what is on his mind at that particular point in time - even though sometimes you might feel that he is taking the long way around the barn to get to his ultimate point.

In fact – Uncle Bob can be counted on to say out loud just EXACTLY what everyone else in the room is quietly thinking.

"Some stories need to be told straight out," Uncle Bob told me once. "And some stories need to be snuck up on and some stories need to be shouted out loud. The only problem is knowing just exactly WHICH stories need to be told straight and which need to be rambled out and snuck up on. In fact there have been more wars and arguments started by folks trying to ramble around a straight out story than a fellow could count on a whole handful of fingers and toes times a whole entire pocketful of pocket calculators."

Yes sir, the man has pure talking talent. I could listen to my Uncle Bob talking all day long – and sometimes I actually have.

Occasionally, I even had a choice in the matter.

But – if you want to boil the truth long enough the simple fact is that my Uncle Bob has taught me nearly everything there is to know about everything important in this world – and he's just getting set to tell me about the rest of it.

Let me give you an example.

Let me tell you about my Uncle Bob's Red Flannel Bible Camp.

This whole thing started when he caught me running away from my Sunday School. I had stuck my hand up and asked to leave the room and then I had gone ahead and left the entire building – namely, our town church – and if I have any sort of say in the matter I might keep on going until I have put an entire continent between me and Sunday School.

You see – I had NEVER really understood that whole concept about having to go to school on a Sunday. I mean I already went five days a week for most of the year. Why in the heck did grown-ups think that a fellow really needed an extra day of schooling?

"I didn't like it in there," I told Uncle Bob. "The preacher kept on talking about loving your enemies and forgiving and such."

"Well, loving and forgiving is important," Uncle Bob said. "Especially when it comes to talking about your enemies."

I shook my head.

"I don't know about that," I said. "Benny Jeeters is always pushing me around at school."

"He's a bully, all right," Uncle Bob said. "His Daddy was before him, too."

"Well how am I supposed to forgive THAT?" I asked. "The way I see it the only way I can truly forgive Benny Jeeters is maybe after I have snucked up behind him with a big old rock and maybe thumped him maybe thirteen or fourteen times – and then I might forgive him with a few kicks to the ribs and maybe show him my new baseball bat about five or six times fast before he could up and surprise-hit me back."

"Is it really a surprise if a fellow sees it coming?" Uncle Bob asked me. "That whole process doesn't sound very sporting to me at all."

"It all depends on hold your mouth while you're doing it," I told him. "He who gets in his first hits fastest doesn't get hit back come the lastest."

Uncle Bob could see the truth in that.

"That still doesn't tell me about why you hate Sunday School so much," Uncle Bob said. "Why don't you try and explain it to me?"

The way I figured it that would take me at least a month of Sundays to properly accomplish – but I figured I had better do my best to explain it to Uncle Bob before he took it into his head to take me back into Sunday School.

"I know all the stories already," I said. "I've heard them at least a hundred times or so. I know that Eve got Adam in trouble by listening to a snake and then Cain hit Abel with a rock and God got upset and rained down buckets and drench-loads for forty days and forty nights and then Moses snuck out of Egypt after drowning the Pharoah and his army in the Red Sea – and I think the Tower of Babel fell down somewhere in between the hello and amen."

"That's pretty close," Uncle Bob told me. "I guess you've been listening."

It was true.

I liked listening to those stories just fine – the first two or three dozen times I went to church and actually listened – but after hearing them told every Sunday year after year after year I just had begun to think that maybe that preacher ought to find himself a whole new book.

"You like going to the library, don't you?" Uncle Bob asked.

"Sure I do," I said. "Books are like television that you can watch without ever having to worry about commercials. Books have special effects and fierce battles and sword fighting and gunplay and bank robbing and dragons and war. Books are cool – all day long."

Some of the kids at school laughed at me about how much I loved books but the simple truth was I would spend a day curled up inside of a book than having a half a dozen birthday parties every year – unless those parties happened to happen inside of a bookstore.

"Well don't you know that all they are talking about in Sunday School is the Bible?" Uncle Bob asked. "And the Bible is one of the best books in the whole wide world?"

I knew about the Bible. Heck, I had even tried to read it once but I got all confused about all of that talk about begetting and smiting and such.

"The Bible is full of battles and death-defying escapes and lions and even a dragon or two. There is war and there are heroes and there is more special effects than you could shake a star cruiser at," Uncle Bob went on.

"Now you're just making stuff up," I said. "I didn't read any of that there."

"I am not making it up," Uncle Bob told me. "Besides, sometimes you have to make up something to get to the truth of what's bothering you."

I wasn't so sure about what he was telling me.

In fact - I was pretty sure that he was just trying to fool me.

Grown-ups will do that to you if you let them get away with it.

"Just let me tell you one of the stories," Uncle Bob said. "In fact I will tell the whole first book to you and then you try and tell me that you don't think that it isn't worth hearing about."

Well, I figured so long as I didn't have to go back into that dry old church that I had nothing to lose by sitting here and giving Uncle Bob's version of the Bible a fair shake.

"This here first book is a story that is called Genesis," Uncle Bob began. "And it goes something like this..."

And then he just kept on talking.

<u>Chapter One – Fiat Lux</u>

"Let there be light," God said – and then all at once there was a bright and calm and peaceful light shining across the entire universe.

God didn't make that light, Uncle Bob went on. He just let us all see it – just the same way as you might let someone else see you smile – which is why I kind of like to think of God as the world's largest light bulb. I suppose you might also think of him as something of a light switch – like he was just turning on the light – but I prefer to think of the light as shining right out of God like it was a part of him that he was allowing us to share in.

Now, just so as you know the rest of this story is going to be ALL my Uncle Bob talking so I am going to do away with all of the quotation marks and the "Uncle Bob said" parts so that you can get right down to the important part of listening and hear it all straight out.

Fiat Lux, Uncle Bob said.

Okay – so that last "Uncle Bob said" snuck out.

I promise I won't interrupt you again.

Fiat Lux is Latin for "Let there be light" – and I know that it sounds like a cross between a sports car and a vacuum cleaner with a bar of soap caught up in its wind-hose and maybe it actually is because light is something that is bright and shiny and faster than anything you could ever think of.

"That's good," God said.

Come the next day - once God could finally see what he was doing he got right down to the business of world-building.

First he raised up a sky just the same way as you or me would raise up a roof over a big old barn that you and I were raising out of a heap of two by fours.

I like to think that he was covering the whole thing over with an umbrella of sky to protect it from spoiling.

"That's good, too," God said.

Then – on the third day, if you are actually keeping count – God just let fly a couple of terrifying terra-firma karate chops, neatly parting the land from the water just as easily as you might part your hair.

Now getting that water separated from that land was important because you can stand upon land but you sure can't stand upon the sea – unless you are wearing a pair of inflatable life jackets for sneakers.

And I know that some of you know-it-alls and read-the-books out there are just dying to reach over and correct what I have just written down and to remind me about that young fellow from Galilee who actually did manage to walk upon the water – but what I am writing and telling you about right now is the Old Testament.

We'll get to that New Testament, by and by.

"That's good, too," God said.

Some of you might also be wondering just why I am talking of light bulbs and race cars way back in a time when things were just getting started and race cars and light bulbs and vacuum cleaners hadn't even been invented yet – but what I am talking about is the word of God – broken down for us ordinary people – and the way I see it the word of God is a kind of be-all and end-all sort of statement.

What I mean to say is that the word of God is timeless – so any anachronisms that you might spot need not actually apply.

Meanwhile – on that very same third day - God got down to the sowing and the planting and he cast down seeds of every kind that you could imagine. Before you knew it grass was growing and trees were branching up out of the dirt and whole fields of cabbage and tomatoes and bluebells and nasturtiums and potatoes started sprouting up like living green shouts of hallelujah come dinnertime.

But not brussel sprouts.

Not even God would touch brussel sprouts.

I don't know just WHO invented brussel sprouts – but he sure wasn't holy.

"That's even better than good," God said, feeling more than a little impressed with himself. "I must be on some kind of a wild lucky roll."

Come the fourth day God decided that he needed a little bit more light and he threw the sun up into the sky and he wired it in good and proper and made sure it was up to the official celestial world-building code of construction and then he decided that he might like something a little calmer – like maybe say a night-light – so he wired in the moon – and then he poked a few holes in the night sky and he decided to call those poke-holes stars and then he strung up a few constellations to give folks something to dream on and then he had himself a cigarette – because even God needs to take a break now and then – and he decided that he would call that cigarette smoke something else.

"Wait a minute," I interrupted. "Are you trying to tell me that God smokes cigarettes?"

"I never said that," Uncle Bob replied. "What I am trying to do is to tell you a story."

I wasn't buying that at all.

"I don't remember hearing anything about cigarettes in the Bible," I said. "I don't remember hearing the preacher mentioning anything about Marlborough country either."

Uncle Bob thought about that.

"Listen," Uncle Bob said. "I am telling you a story – which means that I am using my very own words and thoughts and imagination to do it with. No, it doesn't say anything about God smoking a cigarette in the Bible. I just like to think of him that way is what I am saying."

"Why?" I asked.

"Let's say that you pick up a newspaper tomorrow," Uncle Bob said. "And it's got a story of the President of the United States in

it. Do you think that story is going to mention anything about what the President had for breakfast or whether or not he had a beer or a cigarette before going to bed?"

"No," I said. "I don't imagine the story would have anything to do with what he ate or smoked or drank."

"Of course not," Uncle Bob said. "The story would be about what the President was doing for the country. It would be about him creating this political program or ordering that dam built or this particular war declared. Newspapers – and Bibles – rarely ever concern themselves with what God or the President does with his little time. To them it's more important to talk about what he does with his big world-shaking this-is-what-is-going-to-affect-me-and-other-people sort of time."

That made sense to me.

"Only I'm not writing a newspaper article," Uncle Bob said. "I'm just telling a story about God and what he did back then. That means I get to use my own words and my own voice and my own particular ideas about what God is all about."

I guess I could follow that.

At leastways I told Uncle Bob that I could.

"God created man in his own image," Uncle Bob explained. "So when I tell my stories I like to think about God in my own image as well. It helps me understand him a whole lot more than just sitting down and reading and memorizing a full grown Bible."

"Did you ever even <u>read</u> the Bible?" I asked Uncle Bob.

"I've read it twice in my lifetime," Uncle Bob said. "And I'm reading it – bit by bit – for a third time. But when I tell a story I

am telling it fresh for the very first time ever. And I try to tell it the best way that whoever I am telling it to can understand it."

"So you mean that you're lying about it?" I asked.

"No," Uncle Bob said. "I am not lying about it. What I am doing is telling the story as I like to remember it. You see, to me, those old boys – Adam and Moses and Abraham and Cain – were most likely folks like you or me. They didn't REALLY know that they were supposed to be biblical. They were just trying to get on with their day and do the very best they could – just the same as you or me."

That made sense to me.

"I see God the same way too," Uncle Bob said. "I see him as being just like me – a being who means well and is doing his job the very best way that he knows how."

"So now God has a job?" I asked.

"Of course he does," Uncle Bob said. "He has got a job and he does just as hard and as good as he can do it on account of he is trying to take care of his family – namely, all of us people down here on the planet earth."

"If you say so," I said, still not quite getting it.

"What I am trying to say is that I don't exactly know exactly WHAT God is like," Uncle Bob explained. "All that I know is that I hope God is a little like you or me because at the end of the day I wouldn't feel one bit comfortable with a God who didn't know how to relax and have a smoke and chew the fat at the end of the day."

I guess I understood that a little bit. I always liked to figure that God took time out to read a comic book now and then to –

because even God can enjoy reading about the Hulk dropkicking Superman all over the planet every now and then.

"So God DOESN'T smoke?" I asked.

"How would I know?" Uncle Bob asked with a grin that showed all of his fake teeth and the few real ones that he had left. "I'm just telling a story."

"Now can I get back to telling it?" Uncle Bob asked.

"Go ahead and tell," I told him.

"Clouds," God said. "That makes a whole lot more sense than calling them whooping cranes."

Now some of those heavenly star-holes were nothing more than whoops-goofs and fudge-it-ups where God had either misplaced a nail or banged his thumb with the hammer when he was swinging it.

And yes – even GOD his-own-self occasionally bangs his own thumb.

Once God had done all that sky-building he set the whole thing a-whirling and that there gave us seasons and years and probably gave us income tax as well – but that's okay because all good things come with some sort of a price tag dangling.

You don't believe me – go and ask Minnie Pearl.

So God give us everything – only the one thing that he did not give us no matter how many times people try to blame it on him – was that God did NOT give us religion.

That was something that man made up later.

"Hold it," I said – and I know I promised I wasn't going to interrupt but sometimes a fellow has just got to stick his nose in and ask somebody why something happened. "I thought all along that it was God who INVENTED religion."

Uncle Bob only smiled at that.

"God invented the world and God invented men and women and then God turned us loose and let us be – just the same way as your parents give you a bicycle and told you that you could ride it but they still expect you to keep the tires pumped up."

"Are you saying that God invented responsibility?" I asked.

"How will you ever know what I am saying," Uncle Bob asked. "If you don't let me get back and down to the actual telling?"

Which is EXACTLY what I am going to do, right now.

"That's real good," God said. "I keep this up and folks are going to start to think that I actually knew what I was doing from the first-time out."

Only there wasn't any sort of folks around yet – unless you counted the angels – and even God didn't count the angels because they were way too busy strumming their harps and humming high holy hosannas to bother paying attention to whatever God was up to.

So on the fifth day God got lonely and he decide to create a little wildlife.

So he reached down and he run his fingers through the waters of the oceans and the seas and the lakes and he give those waters a little stir and he created whole teeming swarms of fishes and fat floating forests of algae sprung up from the funk in his fingernails that he had forgotten to clean off from the planting of the day before and every now and then he poked in his thumb and a whole entire flotilla of whales sprouted up.

Then God whistled out a tune and faster than you could say "spit" songbirds flew out of thin air and he whistle a little louder and the big old eagles and the sea gulls and the condors were born and their shadows touched the earth and then the crows and the blackbirds and the ravens took flight from out of those shadows.

I'll tell you a little bit more about those ravens, come Noah time.

Then God snapped his fingers and a dog jumped up and God reached down and he skritched that very first dog directly behind the ears – on account of not even God his-own-self can resist skritching behind a good dog's ears – and before you could say "itch" fleas just sprung naturally into life which just goes to show that even God doesn't always think things through.

Well God he kept on skritching that first dog and before you knew it that old dog was just a'wagging his tail and panting and barking and wriggling – and every time he wagged or panted or barked or wriggled some new animal would be born.

God built up the rabbits and the cattle and the muskrats and the wildebeest and the elephants – who made him giggle and then he skritched out the horses and the buffalo and a ducktailed platypus who made God laugh so loud that he farted and he blamed that on the elephant who hung his head in shame.

"Well that's good, too," God said.

And then God spent the rest of the day sitting there and playing with all of the animals – even the lions and tigers and boa constrictors – and he threw a stick for that dog about two or three thousand times and he drew out a long old tangle of wool from the sheep and he threw that down for the cat to play with.

And it was all good.

Only one thing was missing.

None of these plants and fish and moon and stars and animals could talk worth a rotten bottom-barrel pickle.

God was lonely.

So he got to thinking that he needed just one more thing to make this whole giant planet-wide God-cave absolutely perfect.

Which is most likely when the trouble first got started.

Chapter Two – And God Created Man

"THIS PLACE NEEDS SOME PEOPLE," God said. "I better enliven things up a bit."

So God reached down into the dirt and he piled up a man-sized person out of clay and dust and dirt.

He built a pair of feet for that man to stand on and then he built a funny smell to man's feet so that man could know his up from his down and he could tell which side he was walking on.

"Something's missing," God said. "You can't have a person made out of nothing but feet, now can you?"

So God took a look in his full-sized mirror – because even God needs to know how his hair is looking when he combs it in the morning.

"He needs some legs to move those feet," God said. "And some hipbones to connect those feet to the rest of him."

So God built Man some legs and some hips and a little dangly bit in between those legs, just because he had something left over. He built a chest and a stomach and he filled that chest with a heart that could be filled with love and some lungs that could be filled with air and a gut that could be filled with whatever didn't run fast enough.

Then God screwed on some arms from Man's shoulders and he twist-tied some hands and fingers onto those arms so that Man could keep busy going about God's work or whatever else he figured was worth doing.

Last of all God set a head on top of Man's shoulders.

He tried setting a pumpkin up their first but it just didn't look right. Then he tried using a coconut and a musk-melon but finally he rolled up a ball of clay and he poked a few holes in it and he spit on that clay to give it a little there-you-go and he twisted out a neck so that Man could look around and he popped in a couple of eyeballs so that Man could see what he was doing.

He added ears so that Man could hear when God was talking to him and he whittled out a mouth so that Man could sing God's praises – because even God likes to hear a little music now and then. Next he added hair to keep Man's head warm and he invented dandruff – because even God needs a giggle or two.

The only problem was God was just a little bit tired from all of the heavy-duty creating he had been up to and he made that mouth of Man just a little bit too big which is why most of us tend to talk way too much before we ever get around to thinking about what we are saying and the listening more often than not gets left to the last of it.

Then God took a look at what he had made and he was pretty pleased with how the whole thing had turned out and he leaned down and he planted what looked to be the world's first act of mouth-to-mouth respiration and God breathed soul into the funk and clay and dirt of what he decided he was going to call Man – just because it was easy to spell than xylophone and besides, God had nearly run out of letters after he had finished building up the hippopotamus and the Nova Scotia Duck Tolling Retrievers.

So Man sat up and looked around at what was going on.

"This is all yours," God said. "Just so long as you follow my rules and obey my commands."

"Well this looks pretty good to me," Man said. "And I guess if you want to lay down the law than I can follow it readily enough."

"This here is my Garden," God said. "A garden that I call Eden – and it will be your job to tend to it just as best as you can."

"This is a big old place," Man said. "It might be I could do with a little help of my own, if you could see fit to build up a helping hand.

That made sense to God.

"I guess a matched set wouldn't hurt nothing," God said.

So God figured that wouldn't do any harm so he built himself the very first Woman – only by now God was feeling just a little full of himself – and I guess you couldn't really blame him what with having built up a whole wide world all by himself in seven short days.

So when he got to building this second person he got to feeling a little artsy and he put in some curves that just looked real good and he wrapped a little extra hair around her head and he made her just a little softer in some places and tougher in others and when he was all done with his creating he leaned down and give her a little bit of soul as well.

There's some folks that will tell you that God made women second on account of they are second best – and there are other folks who will tell you that making them second made them BETTER than men because by the second time around God had finally figured out what he was actually doing – but I don't really want to go and open up that particular can of worms right about now – especially seeing as God had only recently invented worms – so all I am going to say on that particular matter is that men and women working together balance things out quite nicely – in my opinion.

"I think I'm going to call her Eve," God said. "On account of I think I have just started something brand new for the very first time."

"Eve sounds good to me," Man said. "Do I get my own name as well?"

Well, like I had said, God was feeling just a little tired by now and it irritated him just a little bit being asked for something more than he had already delivered – especially after creating Eve had been Adam's idea all along - so God swore for the very first time.

"Aw, damn," God said. "If I had known you were going to start asking me for more things just as soon as I had built you I would have let out that whole mouth part of the operation."

Only Man heard different.

When God said "Aw damn", Man heard "Adam" and that was all it took to stick for good.

"Adam," Man said. "That's a good name. That sounds good enough to me."

God didn't see any real need to correct Adam – so he said good enough and left it at that.

"You could hug her now," God suggested. "Seeing as you are supposed to get along together from here on out.

So the next thing you know Adam and Eve up and hugged each other for the very first time.

"You feel pretty good," Adam said.

"You're not so bad yourself," Eve said. "You could use a few sit-ups and crunches– but who's complaining?"

"That's enough of that," God said. "I'm feeling a little tired and I believe I'm going to go and take myself a long old nap – but before I get to napping I want to lay down one law for you to remember."

"You're God," Adam said. "I guess that's what you're good at is laying down the law."

"See that apple tree over in the far acreage?" God asked pointing in the proper direction.

"I see it," Adam said.

"Me too," Eve said.

"You stay away from that tree," God said. "You can climb and chop and pick from any tree there is but just stay away from that one on account of it's my favorite tree."

And then – on that seventh day – God walked off and had himself a good long nap.

"Good bye, God," Adam said, waving as God walked off.

Eve was waving too, but she was thinking about the taste of apples.

Which is where ALL of the trouble first got started.

Chapter Three – Hello Mister Snake

NOW A WHOLE LOT OF PEOPLE who have heard this story will have most likely fallen into the grievous misconception that God is actually telling you that women are weak and can't be trusted and will most likely get up to some kind of mischief if you leave them unsupervised for just a little bit too long.

That isn't necessarily the case – and I'll explain it as I go.

"I like this garden," Adam told Eve. "Mind you, it could use a color television set and possibly a hook-up to the sports network and some beer wouldn't hurt none – but other than that I like it just fine. We have got all of the vegetables that we care to eat and a dog to skritch and a cat who stays just far enough away from a fellow to make you have to lean over and bend down to skritch him if he lets you. We have got birds to sing to us and sheep to baa at us and a moose to stand in the swamp and look funny and even though I couldn't really tell what the heck was up with that duckbilled platypus I still like our garden just fine."

"Maybe so," Eve said. "But don't you ever wonder just what those apples might taste like on that Forbidden Tree?"

You see – that's where that whole misconception about women being weak and easy to tempt first got started. The sad fact is though, women aren't all that weaker than we fellas are. The fact is even though God made us bigger and stronger he also gave women a few more brain cells than us men. Eve wasn't thinking about mischief or messing around with Adam's state of existence. Eve was thinking about possibility and finding out why something was.

See the way I see it - women were built to wonder.

And – once a body gets to wondering, sooner or later they are bound to wander and Eve she just went and wandered on over to that big old Forbidden Tree and when she got there she saw that she wasn't alone. There was a little-bitty old snake hanging in the branches of that tree and he smiled and he stuck his tongue out at Eve – which would have been rude for anybody else but when you are a snake sticking out your tongue is just sort of how you say howdy.

And it was a REALLY pretty little snake – small and soft and colored like all of the rainbows of the world shook down into a glass full of magic multi-flavor milkshake and stirred with a box of Crayola color crayons.

"What are you doing way over on this side of the garden?" that pretty little snake asked Eve. "I never saw you here before."

"I just come for a look," Eve said. "I wanted to see what was the great big deal about all of these apples over here."

"I'm right glad you came on over here," the pretty little snake said. "Because I've been getting so lonesome that I was about to start talking to the rocks and the dirt and they aren't much on conversational ability."

Now what Eve didn't know – and what you would know if you had actually gone to and stayed in Sunday School just long enough to learn something – was that old snake was actually the Devil himself in disguise.

I'm not really all that sure just why the Devil figured disguising himself as a snake was all that smart of a thing to do but I kind of have a sneaking sort of suspicion that he was just trying to save a little money on shoe leather. I mean everyone knows that snakes don't need shoes because their hide is so tough and smooth – which is why so many folks like to wear a pair of snake-skin boots.

In fact, the more I think on it the more I believe that I might actually be onto something with that particular theory. I mean ALL of the story books talk about how that old Devil is always hankering and bargaining for soles – so many he does have some weird sort of Mephistophelean shoe fetish.

"Did you ever wonder why that sky is so blue?" the Devil Snake asked Eve. "I mean it could have been green or coffee-colored or magenta or even paisley. Just why do you think it decided to be blue?"

"Well that's a pretty good question," Eve said. "I don't really think I know the answer to it unless maybe it's just sad or something."

"How about why a rock falls into the dirt when you drop it?" the Devil Snake asked. "Why do you figure that happens?"

"Well, I don't rightly know," Eve replied.

"How about the wind?" the Devil Snake asked. "What makes the wind blow here and there like it does? Do you know the answer to that question?"

"Well, Adam always says it's on account of God ate too many baked beans for his supper," Eve said. "But Adam always grins just a little too hard when he says that to me so I'm pretty sure he's just making that whole thing up."

The snake snorted loudly.

"I know exactly the reason why all those things happen the way they do," the Devil Snake said. "On account of I've been eating on these here apples. You see, apples are brain food – which is why you are supposed to bring one to your teacher - and this here is a right smart tree full of properly-educated apples and if you were to reach up and take yourself just a single bite of one of these apples I bet you'd be smarter quicker than you could say spit."

The Devil Snake kept at it all day long, talking himself in circles trying his hardest and best to convince Eve to take just a single bite of that apple - and finally she did.

She reached out and she pulled down an apple and she took herself a big old bite.

"Tastes good, doesn't it?" the Devil Snake asked.

"It does," Eve admitted. "But I still don't know why the sky is blue."

"Maybe it takes some time," the Devil Snake said. "Why don't you take another bite while you're at it?"

Meanwhile that old Devil Snake had started to swell up, even fatter and larger and meaner looking.

"I'm beginning to think that you are tricking me," Eve said.

Meanwhile, all of those magical pretty colors that snake had been showing her darkened and muddied like a summer sky clouding over into rain.

"See," the Devil Snake answered. "You're smarter already."

Then he stuck his tongue at her – only this time he wasn't saying anything like Howdy – and Eve ran off to get Adam.

Now this is where a lot of storytellers get things wrong with this story. Most folks will tell you how Eve tempted Adam with that apple, dangling it under his nose and telling him just how good it was going to taste and teasing him about how a big old man like him was scared of doing something that a woman had already done.

Only that isn't quite the way that things happened.

I mean think about it.

If you're a pretty woman and you want to tempt a man you sure don't have to wave no freshly-picked apple under his nose – unless maybe you are promising to bake that apple into a big old apple pie.

Now I'm hungry, darn it.

Well, while I sit here thinking about hot apple pie with a wedge of funky old rat trap cheese and a tall glass of cold white milk, why don't I tell you just how that whole apple-tempting situation all played out?

The way that it happened was this.

"I'm in big trouble," Eve told Adam. "I had me a bite of that forbidden apple."

Well, old Adam he decided that if Eve was in trouble he wasn't going to leave her hanging there on her all-alone-lonesome so he took that apple from her and he bit right down onto it and he chewed up just as much as she had – and maybe even a little bit more on account of it WAS a pretty good apple – and like I said, Adam had himself an AWFULLY big old mouth.

"God is going to get angry with us," Eve said. "We just broke his number one rule."

"He got to find us first," Adam said. "Let's hide ourselves behind these leaves."

So Adam and Eve made themselves the first ever camouflage suit out of a bushel or two of leaves and grass but God spotted them just the same.

"Why'd you eat my apple off of my favorite apple tree?" God asked. "I told you not to."

"That there snake tricked me," Eve said.

"I took a bite too," Adam said, sticking up for Eve. "If you want to blame her you better blame me too."

Which was right about when that Devil-Snake showed up again – only this time he was laughing and he was grinning at God and he had swollen up large enough to make an anaconda look mostly puny. He had grown wings and he was blowing fire out of his mouth and he had turned himself into something that looked a lot less like a snake and a whole lot more like a big old mean-spirited dragon.

So God went to that Devil-Snake and he hit him so hard that he broke all of the snake's teeth but two of them and along the way God's left-most knuckle split that old snake's tongue like a silver dinner fork. Then God stepped on that snake hard enough to leave tread marks – which is why a snake has so many scales.

"That'll learn you," God said.

"I feel smarter already," the Devil Snake said, shrinking down and slithering back into the shadows from where he had first come from.

Then God turned his wrath on Adam and Eve who were waiting for God to hit and step on them.

"I trusted you two and then you paid me back when you went and you broke my trust so this here is an eviction notice and you two are going to have to get out of Eden before the sun goes down to bed."

So Adam and Eve packed up their belongings – which weren't much more than that bushel or two of leaves and grass – and they walked out of Eden with their heads held high and I kind of like to think that God had maybe figured on that and he was grinning too – only you couldn't see much behind that old boy's two bushel chin full of beard.

Now I can hear some of you out there moaning and going on about how this wasn't really fair and why was God kicking Adam and Eve out of their own home just for eating an apple – but you've got to stop your moaning and going on just long enough to think about the whole entire situation.

Besides, life is WAY too short for wasting it on indignation.

Just take a look at the big picture.

The fact is – God was kind of like a parent to Adam and Eve – and the very best thing a parent can do for their children is to tell them that it is time for them to go out into the world and to find their own destiny.

So God wasn't being mean or unfair.

God was just teaching those two young kids how to stand up on their own two feet.

"Where will we go now?" Eve asked. "We sure can't go back."

"We will go east from Eden," Adam said. "We'll just have to follow our nose and we'll make our own way as we go."

To make sure they couldn't sneak back in to Eden, God stationed a pair of fierce-looking angels with a big giant flaming sword that looked scary enough to discourage any sort of break and entry – but between you and me and those two big scary angels – God left a little eternity-candle burning just in back of that big old flaming sword on account of – in his heart of hearts – he always hoped that one day his children would make their way back home to Eden.

Parents never really learn, do they?

Chapter Four – Some Unanswered Questions

ALL RIGHT — SO I PROMISED that I wasn't going to interrupt but just the same I have to.

"You said there was going to be some battles," I said to Uncle Bob.

"Those battles come a little further on."

"You also said something about swordfights and gunplay," I pointed out.

"There was a sword," Uncle Bob said. "And it was flaming, too."

A flaming sword was pretty exciting – but not when it was standing there hovering in front of a garden gate.

I told Uncle Bob that too.

"The swordfights are coming up down the road," Uncle Bob said. "The Bible is a big old set of stories and you've just taken one step on a long old road."

I still wasn't convinced.

"What about them special effects you promised me?"

"What?" Uncle Bob asked. "Building a whole world and a giant flaming sword and a snake turning into a dragon wasn't special enough of an effect for you?"

"Not hardly," I said.

"Well, if you want to you can sit and listen just a little bit longer and I will tell you the rest of the story – the way I know it, anyways," Uncle Bob said. "I think if you've got the patience for it you'll find there's plenty to be excited about in the next couple of chapters."

"Like what?"

"Like a murder," Uncle Bob said. "That's always exciting, isn't it?"

I thought about that.

"Well, if I had patience I'd probably be a doctor," I sassed right back. "But you just keep on talking. There's nothing on television worth watching so I might as well give you a little more of a listen-to."

"I feel so special," Uncle Bob said. "What with knowing that you're going to deign to listen to me."

"What's deign?" I asked.

"A fellow who grew up in Denmark," Uncle Bob answered. "If you want to listen you better swallow a couple of those question marks that keep peeking out from behind your teeth."

Which is just exactly what I did. I sat and I listened.

And Uncle Bob kept on telling.

Chapter Five – Comes A Murder

WELL LET ME TELL YOU - the countryside East of Eden was one long old hot stretch of pure and utter desolation.

The sand was hard and there were more rocks than a fellow could count with a fistful of pocket calculators and a truckload of abaci but Adam and Eve made out just as best they could. They found a valley and they built themselves a little home and they had two male children named Cain and Abel.

For a time, Adam and Eve were about as happy as you could imagine.

Well, maybe Eve was even happier. She was so darned happy that one of the first things she did after giving birth to Cain was to look up into the heavens and say "With God's help I have given birth to a man-child."

After which Adam was heard to mutter to himself something about "You know, it might be that I had more than just a little to do with that whole procedure myself."

That didn't stop Eve from saying mostly about the same sort of thing when Abel was born – but she said it a little bit more quieter so as not to go hurting poor old Adam's feelings. By now she had figured out that even though men are most generally bigger and stronger than women – we have thinner skins when it comes to self-esteem.

Hey – they call it "ego", not "she-go".

Now Cain was tall and dark haired. He was even beginning to sport a bit of a peach-fuzzy chin scraggle that almost nearly passed for a half of a beard – if you squinted. He had thirteen hairs on his chest that he counted every morning. Every night he would water those chest hairs with a little water from the stream a little bit of horse manure on account of he figured if it would make crops grow it would work chest hair too. He kept at it every night – just hoping and praying that those chest hairs would maybe take the hint and would up and grow themselves a few more brothers and sisters.

Mostly sisters – on account of women were still awfully scarce in this new land that his Mom and Dad had taken him too. I expect that was part of the reason for Cain's growing jealousy of his brother Abel.

You know how it is sometimes.

Even when there isn't a single shred of evidence that your Mom and your Dad feel the way that you think they do there is still something dark and mean and nasty that grows down deep in a young boy's heart – something that slithers and curls and twines around his darkest thoughts like a low-growing snake – whispering to that young boy night after night that his parents love his younger brother a whole lot more than they love him.

"Things were better before you came along," Cain would sometimes tell Abel.

Only that REALLY wasn't the truth of it.

Cain just tried a little too hard, was all.

You know the type of guy I mean. The kind of guy that goes WAY beyond over-achieving. I am talking about the kind of fellow who would use a sixteen pound sledgehammer to crack open a freshly-laid hummingbird egg. I am talking about the kind of fellow who yells when he ought to be whispering, who jumps when he ought to just take a single careful step – the kind of fellow who throws a rock when he really ought to just wave hello.

The fact is that Cain was that certain kind of fellow who couldn't even SPELL the word careful. He just plain thought too fast and moved too hard and he just wouldn't ever learn to keep his big scraggle-bearded mouth shut.

Cain was just that kind of fellow.

I can't really tell you if it was his father's fault or his mother's fault or if he just plain grew that way in the first place. Maybe it was the way that God built him. I can't rightly tell you why it was – it just was is all. Trying to figure out what made Cain the way he was is a little bit like standing in the middle of a forty-acre forest fire while the flames are roaring over your head and trying to figure just who dropped the first lit match.

The only thing that really seemed to make Cain happy was growing things in the dirt. You know just how some people are sort of born with a green thumb? Well, Cain was green all over from head to toe. Green with envy and green with vegetable talent. Without a word of a lie he could drop a seed into the dirt and spit on it and by the morning an entire field of beets would have grown up overnight.

Abel was the complete other side of the coin. He didn't care much for crops and grain and growing things. The way Abel figured it dirt was just way too quiet for his liking. Abel loved to sing and he played the flute and he loved to raise sheep on account of he could sing to them all day long and the worst they might say in reply was "baa".

Like I told you, Cain was the whole other way entirely.

He never laughed unless it was at something mean that he had seen.

In fact, I don't really think that Cain even knew how to smile.

You know the type – all dark and gloomy and intense. The kind of guy who just looks at you when you say something funny and then says something mean and gloomy – like "Well, that was a really dumb thing to say."

Like I told you – Cain was mean enough to steal a dead fly from a stone-blind spider and then laugh while the little arachnid starved to death.

Worse thing was - about the only topic that Cain REALLY cared to talk about was the state of his crops.

That boy could talk fertilizer like it was nobody's business. He could tell you about the time of day that you ought to plant your root crops. He could tell you whether it was going to rain that day – even if there wasn't a single cloud in the sky. He could tell you by the turn of a leaf whether or not a certain given plant was going to grow healthy or strong.

Yes sir, Cain was a farmer, plain and simple.

Now I am not saying that there is anything wrong in being a farmer but being obsessed with it like Cain was obsessed with it was NEVER a good idea.

It sure didn't help much with any sort of brotherly bonding.

You see, like I told you Abel was a shepherd – and for him the only reasonable use for anything growing in the dirt was to feed his flock of sheep with – and as far as Cain was concerned those sheep did nothing more useful than chew down the grass and hoof up the dirt.

Oh sure, they were all right with mint jelly – but after that Cain had absolutely no use for sheep whatsoever.

So as you can imagine Cain and Abel were sort of destined to NOT get along with each other. They went together worse than milk and pickles.

Normally that wouldn't have been a problem.

I mean siblings aren't SUPPOSED to get along.

The trouble REALLY got started with the sacrifice.

You see – Adam told his sons that they ought to be putting some thought into making some sort of a sacrifice to the Lord God Jehovah.

"He likes that sort of thing," Adam told his sons. "I guess I can't really blame him. Everybody loves the smell of a good barbecue."

"I will do that," Abel said. "I will do that because my father told me to."

Abel ALWAYS listened to what his father told him.

Cain he wasn't so sure about what his Daddy was telling him.

"Let me think on that," Cain said. "I'm not quite sure that what you're telling me is making any real kind of sense."

Meanwhile Abel didn't waste any time.

He went down to his herd of sheep and he picked out the fattest juiciest lamb that he could find.

He took a sharp knife and he sacrificed that lamb and then he lit himself a fire and he put those lamb chops on the fire and he said a little sheepish prayer of gratitude and before you could say "Smucker's Mint Jelly" a couple of proud-looking angels flew down and told Abel that God had said that he'd done right some good with his sacrifice.

Cain heard what had happened and he got to feeling right cantankerous about the whole darned situation.

"I'll show that brother of mine how to make a sacrifice," Cain said. "He hasn't seen ANYTHING yet."

So old Cain he went out into the woods and he found himself the tallest tree that he could find and he took out his axe and he hacked and he hacked and he hacked at that tree until he came down and hit the dirt hard.

That was Cain at his best, you understand.

Hitting and hacking and making a mess out of a perfectly good tree.

By then Cain should have tired all of that anger out of his spirit but all of that hard work just made him arch his back and his shoulders knotted up like a mule in a hailstorm.

"I'll show him," he kept whispering to himself.

The madder he got the stronger he got.

The fact of it is Cain could have basically given mad-strong lessons to the Incredible Hulk himself.

Cain hacked off the sturdiest limbs he could find and then he dragged them back to the rock where Abel had made his sacrifice.

"I'll show him. I'll show him."

Steam locomotives had not been invented yet – but if they HAD you can bet your top and bottom dollar that if anyone had heard Cain coming through the woods hissing and muttering about how he was going to show up his brother Abel than they would have sworn that there was a full-blown steam locomotive barreling through those woods.

"I'll show him, I'll show him, I'll show him."

And the more that Cain muttered and hissed and whispered and growled the angrier he got.

He dug up ten great rocks and he laid them one on top of each other – only stubbing his thumbs once or twice or fifteen times.

Which didn't help his disposition one little bit.

Then Cain laid a big old heap of turnips and parsnips and beets and green tomatoes and scallions on top of that top most rock.

While he was doing that Cain took great care to single out the moldiest and most worm-eaten vegetables he could find.

"If all I am going to do is just burn them on a fire," Cain told himself. "I might as well burn the rotten vegetables and keep the good ones for myself."

That greediness – more than anything else – was what decided just exactly what would happen next.

Cain heaped up all of the firewood that he had hacked from off of that big tall tree and he slapped a chunk of flint until he had sparked up a fire and that firewood caught and faster than you could say stew-without-beef those vegetables began to burn.

A mean dark cloud of smoke rose up like a long evil snake crawling up towards the general direction of heaven and a reek that stank like the worst part of perdition, come house-cleaning day.

Now I am NOT trying to let on that the Good Lord has anything against eating his vegetables but the way that sacrifice reeked was something that had to be smelled to be believed. God took one quick look down while holding his nose like his hands had grown clothespins. Then he shook his head like he was trying to shake off a bad dream – and then he sent down a big old rainstorm that drowned out Cain's sacrificial fire.

"You're going about it the wrong way," Abel said to his brother. "Didn't you hear Daddy saying that we ought to make ourselves a blood-sacrifice? The way I heard it he wasn't saying anything about no turnip-sacrifice."

Which didn't help the situation much at all – but Abel was only trying to be nice. In fact he even went as far as to offer Cain one of his next-best sheep so that Cain could make himself a proper meat sacrifice.

Only Cain wasn't hearing any of that.

"I'll show you what a blood sacrifice looks like," Cain said darkly. "You come on to the field with me and I'll show you something that will REALLY open up your mind."

Too bad Abel was such a trusting soul.

He went out into the field with Cain and then Cain fetched up a melon-sized rock and come up behind his brother Abel when he wasn't looking and he stove his brother's skull in with two or three swings of that rock.

The next thing you know Cain was standing there looking down at the dead body of his brother Abel.

That's right.

You heard it from me first.

Cain had gone and invented murder.

Next thing he invented was an alibi – throwing in a little self-denial to keep his thinking nicely muddled.

"Nobody saw me do anything," Cain told himself. "There is absolutely no reason on earth that Mom or Dad is going to blame me. I can just tell them that my brother Abel fell down two or three times and hit his head on that rock."

He did have a point.

I mean what were they going to do – go all C.S.I. on a rock?

Only Cain forgot about one key witness.

God was looking.

And he had seen the whole thing.

Chapter Six – Murder Will Out

CAIN WAS RIGHT ABOUT ONE THING.

His parents didn't want to see what he had gone and done to his brother.

I mean just think about it.

You've got two sons.

The only two sons in the world and one of them turns up dead.

Are you REALLY going to be in all that much of a hurry to lay blame on the last son you got left to your name?

So – if it had been left up to Adam and Eve most likely Cain would have got away with what he had gone and done.

Only God stepped in.

See, God was watching the whole time.

I know that some of you might be wondering just why God didn't do anything about what Cain was up to – but that wasn't the way that God operated.

Not then and not now.

You see, God is a REAL big believer in free will.

He wants his children to make up their own minds – but don't you be fooled into calling that any kind of indifference.

The fact is, God is ALWAYS watching.

And he cares about what he sees.

So he saw what Cain did and it got him in the same way that it might get to you or me.

God felt bad.

"Hey Cain," God shouted out. "What are you doing down there with that big old rock in your hand?"

Cain didn't answer.

He heard God – just the same way as you might hear a thunderstorm going off in your good left ear – but he just took off running and he went and hid himself under a big old boulder.

"He'll never find me here," Cain told himself.

Only that big old boulder didn't fool God one little tiny bit.

"I see you hiding under that rock, Cain. Where's your brother Abel got to?" God asked. "I'm hankering for a few more of those lamb chops he cooked up."

Cain thought fast.

"How the heck would I know?" Cain asked God. "Am I my brother's keeper?"

Now I know – that wasn't exactly the smartest thing to say. I mean – if you ask me – right about then I would be thinking about asking to see my lawyer or maybe pleading the fifth or at the very least saying that some other guy had gone and done it.

But no sir – all that Cain could think of to say was – "Am I my brother's keeper?"

I said that Cain was mean.

I never told you that he was bright.

"You want to try running that by me one more time?" God asked. "Or do you REALLY figure I wasn't going to see what you've been up to?"

Cain stuttered and stammered but no matter how hard he tried his story stank worse than that heap of burning rotten vegetables.

"I can hear the blood of Abel calling up from out of the field where you struck him down," God said to Cain. "It's hurting my ears it cries so loudly."

By now Cain could hear it too – and he felt bad for what he had gone and done – but there wasn't any going back from what had already happened.

So God reached down and he popped Cain right in the eye and that eye-bruise swelled up all black and nasty like the mother of all thunderclouds.

"That's going to leave a mark," God said. "And that mark is how people will know you. From here on out you are cursed by the Lord. You must leave your home and you must go out into the wilderness and you will plant no more because whatever you try and grow will taste as bitter as a glass full of freshly-cried tears."

And so, just as Cain's parents had been given an eviction notice from out of the Garden of Eden Cain also had to get the heck out of Dodge. He fled to a land called Nod and there he met and fell in love with and married the first woman who would have him.

I guess beggars can't be choosers.

Now I can hear you asking "If Adam and Eve were the first two people where'd this other woman come from?"

Well, the fact is this is a big old world. You know it and I know it and you can bet your bottom shekel that God knew it too. And it just stands to reason that he would look down at this big old world that he had built and he would start to make a few more people to fill it up with – just the same way as you might look at a bookshelf with two single books on it and get to thinking about just how many books you could buy and keep on that big old empty shelf.

Just take my word on it – there was another woman and Cain met her and married her.

What was her name?

Man, you've got more questions than a barrel full of Wikipedia.

I don't KNOW her name.

It never said in the Bible.

Anyways – to make a long story short Cain and this nameless woman got busy begetting – and I'm not about to explain "begetting" and "begatting" to you.

You're just going to have go and Google it if you REALLY want to know.

Before too long Cain and this woman had begotten themselves a son that Cain decided to name Enoch. Then Cain built himself a town – most likely on account of he couldn't be a farmer any longer so he might as well turn himself into a city slicker. He named that town Enoch after his son and life was comfortable.

Well, Enoch grew up and met another woman and he and she begat themselves a son that they called Irad and then he grew up and begat himself a son that he called Mehujael and Mehujael begat HIMSELF a son that he called Methushael – NOT to be confused with Methuselah – whom I'll tell you about just a little bit later.

Now there was an awful lot of begetting going on there for a while.

I mean, what else was there to do?

Cable television hadn't been invented yet.

Neither had Angry Birds.

Just let me tell you all about it.

Chapter Seven – Beginning the Begetting

MEANWHILE — WHILE CAIN AND "THAT NOD WOMAN" were busy begetting Enoch – Adam and Eve were getting busy with a little begetting of their own.

You see – Adam and Eve begot Seth – which was a pretty good trick when you stop and think that according to the Bible Adam was about 130 years old at the time that he and Eve got around to begotting Seth – but maybe folks ate better back then.

Seth found himself a wife – whose name has mostly been forgotten by biblical historians – and between her and Cain's wife I'm not really sure WHAT that says about what the Bible thinks about women who came after Eve.

So Seth and his wife begot ENOS or ENOSH as he is sometimes called by those folks who are more readily embarrassed than I am.

For the statistically-minded of you Seth lived to 912 years old – according to Biblical census takers.

A short time later old Enos found himself a wife and they begot CAINAN or KENAN – depending on how you hold your mouth while you are spelling it.

Cainan – or Kenan – met and married up with "some" woman and after ANOTHER hundred years or so they successfully begat a son they named MAHALALEL – which I defy you to say five or ten times fast without sliding into a rousing chorus of the "la-la-la" song.

Enos was about ninety years old – according to Biblical scholars – when he and that "some" woman gave birth to Cainan – or Kenan.

Enos died at the age of 905.

Cainan – or Kenan - according to Bible scholars – had his first and only son – Mahalalel – when he was 70 years old and then Kenan died at the way-past-ripe old age of 910 years.

Shoot, cinnamon and Sylvester Stallone – I know darn well that I should have written myself a flow chart or something like that. You might want to keep some cheat sheets handy if you're starting to lose track.

So Mahalalel – son of Kenan, grandson of Enos, great-grandson of Seth, great-great-grandson of Adam – (who came first) – helped "some" woman give birth to JARED and live a mere 895 years.

Next thing you know Jared – son of Mahalalel, grandson of Kenan, great-grandson of Enos, great-great-grandson of Seth, great-great-great-grandson of Adam – (who came first) – helped "some" woman give birth to ENOCH – not to be confused with Enoch, the son of Cain.

Jared died at 962 years old.

I'm not going to say much about him in case the folks at Subway are listening in on this storytelling situation.

Meantime ENOCH – son of Jared, grandson of Mahalalel, great-grandson of Kenan, great-great-grandson of Enos, great-great-great-grandson of Seth – who was the great-great-great-great-grandson of Adam (who came first) found himself in bed with "some woman" and after living for "some centuries" God "took him" – which goes to show you that Biblical scorekeepers must have been particularly slack around that particular era.

But not before Enoch (the great-great-great-great-grandson of Adam – who came first) and that aforementioned "some woman" gave birth to METHUSELAH – the oldest man in the known biblical universe.

Methuselah who lived to be 969 years old – which is 239 in dog years – which is a heck of a long time no matter how you count it – but maybe he was just being careful, is all. For those of you statistical-minded people out there – haven't you got some randomly scattered mustard seeds that desperately need to be counted?

Anyway, Methuselah – son of Enoch, grandson of Jared, great-grandson of Mahalalel, great-great-grandson of Kenan, great-great-great-grandson of the unfortunately-named Enos, great-great-great-great-grandson of Seth, great-great-great-great-great-grandson of Adam (who came first) got together with one more of them "some women" and fathered Lamech – the son of Methuselah, grandson of Enoch, great-grandson of Jared, great-great-grandson of Mahalalel, great-great-great-grandson of Kenan, great-great-great-great-grandson of Enos, great-great-great-great-great-grandson of Seth, great-great-great-great-grandson of Adam (who came first).

And then along came Noah.

Chapter Eight – An Author's Aside on Anonymous Women

NOW – BEFORE I MOVE MUCH FURTHER down the road on this Bible Class reading I feel like I ought to explain my whole viewpoint on that oddly prevalent theme of "some women".

You see – I am a writer – and as such I have a keen eye regarding the importance of proper research.

So it disturbs when I come across undocumented hearsay literature – so the astounding prevalence of unknown participants in Biblical history truly irritates me.

Let me go over a bit of a list for you.

We've got Cain's wife.

No name.

We've got Adam and Eve's two daughters – totally nameless but mentioned in some archaic Biblical tomes.

We've got the aforementioned wife of Seth, not to mention the unmentioned wife of Kenan and Enos and the anonymous wife of Halelalel – who most likely died of a bad case of terminal tongue-twist.

Still anonymous.

We've got Jared and Enoch and umpteen-year Methuselah and Lamech, who fathered Noah.

None of their wives names were worth recording.

Then we've got Noah himself – who I will tell you all about in the very next chapter. He was married and Biblical historians never saw fit to bother writing down HER name at all. I mean just think about it. Didn't the old codger even bother to send his wife a Valentine's Day card?

He probably saved all of his money to build himself that boat.

But I'm getting ahead of myself.

You might also want to throw in Ham's wife and his daughter and the wife of Nimrod and the mother of Abraham.

All four of them ingloriously nameless.

Not to mention Lot's wife and Lot's daughters and Laban's wife and Potiphar's wife and the wife of the Pharoah – man, you think a power-wife like thought ought to have SOME sort of publicity wouldn't you?

Nope, nope, nope and nope.

Nameless women, one and all.

You might argue that the Pharoah's magicians didn't have names either but were most likely men but that argument doesn't hold much water with me. Heck,, court magicians are SUPPOSED to be mysterious so it's really no surprise at all they would opt for a murky incognito-dom.

Then there is Simeon's wife and Moses wife and Job's wife – imagine what SHE had to put up with.

More "some women".

More anonymous roll-callers.

Now I am NOT a feminist by any stretch of the imagination – but it makes me wonder how did all of these unnamed women escape baptism?

Might be old John the Baptist was falling down on the job.

Then there is Samson's mother and Haman's mother and Jepthah's mother David's mother and the Witch of Endor – heck, she had a title and she still wasn't consider worthy of a name.

Maybe witches are supposed to be mysterious as well.

Are you keeping count?

Not even the QUEEN OF SHEBA was deemed worthy of a name.

I could go on.

I haven't even touched the New Testament yet.

But I don't really want to make too much of a fuss about it.

The main thing to remember is that God didn't really write the Bible – he was way too busy living in it. The fellows who wrote the Bible – and I bet you my last two hundred dollars that they were MOSTLY if not ALL fellows – probably didn't think too much of the worth of a woman beyond the all-too-usual "Hey honey, can you make me a quick grilled cheese sandwich?"

Besides that – we were talking about Noah - and old what's-her-name, Noah's wife.

Chapter Nine - Noah's Many-Storied Ark

LIKE YOU'VE SEEN IN THAT LAST CHAPTER or two there was an awful lot of begetting getting done after Adam and Eve checked out of Eden.

The Earth began to fill up with people and that is always a recipe for trouble.

You have two people over for supper and the worst you've got to look forward to is a little dispute over politics halfway through the pecan pie. But if those two dinner guests bring along twenty other friends you know for a fact that sooner or later SOMEBODY is going to burn the house down around your ears.

That's the whole problem with free will, now isn't it?

Sooner or later people start thinking up things.

Before you know it they are talking about turning away from God. They start coveting their neighbor's wives and lying and cheating and murdering each other just as quick as you can chuck a rock.

Next thing you know we've got taxes and surveys.

"God?" they'll say. "What sort of God are you talking about?"

The next thing you know they are worshiping the sun and the stars and the planets. They are making up gods just to explain away things that happen to them.

Say some fellow goes out walking in the rain and he forgets to bring along his rubber boots and umbrella.

"Oh," that fellow will tell you. "That was all the rain-god's fault. He's the real problem here – not me."

Or say some other fellow steals another fellow's wallet.

"Oh," that thieving other fellow will tell you. "That was just the god of thieves fault. He made me do it. I didn't have any sort of say in the matter."

Sooner or later we all will grin and tell you that the devil made us burn your house down.

Before you know it, people start drinking hard liquor and getting into fist fights and generally being all-around un-Christian-like and before you know it sin creeps in and they start doing terrible things.

At least that's how Noah saw it.

"This isn't how things are supposed to be," Noah would tell folks whenever he saw them getting up to no good. "You people really shouldn't ought to be doing things like that."

Which didn't help matters much.

"Well who asked you to watch us while we are doing it?" those people would ask Noah right on back. "Why don't you just go and look in some other direction?"

But no matter what direction Noah looked in – all that he could see was badness and no good and it filled his heart with a deep dark despair.

"What can I do about this sort of thing?" Noah asked "some woman" – namely, his wife.

"Honey," his wife would tell him. "You really ought to try and relax. You're five hundred years old now. It is time that you realized that things just aren't the way that they were back when you were a kid."

Which was true, sadly enough.

Noah WAS five hundred years old – but he had still managed to father three sons named Shem, Ham and Japheth – and some daughters as well.

Let me tell you a little bit about Noah's family.

First off there was Shem.

Shem was the oldest son – and by this time of his life he had met and married "some woman" and the two of them had begatted five sons – namely Elam, Asshur, Arphaxad, Lud, Aram and "some daughters".

Ham was the middle child – which is often a recipe for trouble.

Early on in Ham's life he had caught his daddy Noah while Noah was testing the harvest of his newly-planted vineyard just a little too intensely. The way that some people tell it Ham caught Noah getting naked while he was drunk on wine and

Noah had cursed at him some but none of that prevented from growing up and getting married to "some woman" and fathering four sons – namely Cush, Mizraim, Phut and Canaan.

"I whole-heartedly blame myself," Noah later noted. "It serves me right for naming a son after a breakfast choice."

Meanwhile the youngest brother – Japheth – had met up and married with "some OTHER woman" and the two of them had raised up at least SEVEN sons - Gomer, Magog, Tiras, Javan, Meshech, Tubal, and Madai.

Now this whole mess of sons and grandsons and some women and some daughters all lived together with Noah and his wife – which meant that they ALL had to listen to old Noah moaning and going on about the evils and wickedness of people these days.

This went on until every night God had to listen to Noah's wife and his sons and his daughters and his daughter-in-laws all praying that somebody was going to do SOMETHING about all of Noah's griping and complaints.

Which was an awful lot of prayers to have to listen to – so God got up out of his own bed and looked down in the nighttime and called out to Noah.

"Hey Noah," God said.

God was always a little informal like that. I know that a lot of Biblical authors will tell you how God was always going on about thou shalt and shalt not – but folks who really know will tell you that God was good people.

"Who's that?" Noah asked.

"It's God," God said.

"That's a likely story," Noah replied. "This is some kind of a telemarketing scam, isn't it? You're going to tell me that I've won some sort of a cruise, aren't you?"

"Well, as a matter of fact," God said, with a quiet little Godly chuckle. "You're pretty close to being nearly right."

"I knew it," Noah said. "So what's the hitch? What do I got to do to get me some peace and quiet around here?"

God laughed a little at that.

"I've been watching," God said. "And I ain't too happy with what I have been seeing. All of these people sinning and getting all rowdy and up to no good. It seems to me that you and your family are about the only good people left on this world."

"That's what I've been trying to tell people," Noah said. "So why don't you tell me something that I <u>don't</u> already know?"

"I'm going to do just that," God said. "If you'll give me half a chance to get around to telling it to you."

"You're going to tell me something that I don't already know?" Noah asked. "Go ahead, I'm all ears."

"Brace yourself," God said to Noah. "I am going to by-all-that's-holy end this world – once and for all."

"Well that's awfully bad news," Noah replied. "Seems a shame to destroy the whole place after you went and took seven wholo days to build it "

"I'm not talking about destroying it," God said. "I've just got to give a good old wash over, is all. There is nothing that a little water and elbow grease won't cure."

"So which part do I have to provide?" Noah asked.

"I already told you that I was providing the water," God said. "You get to provide the elbow grease."

"That figures," Noah said. "Lucky me."

"First off," God said. "I want you to make me a big old ark out of cypress wood – which is nice and waterproof. Then I want you to make rooms in it and coat the whole thing with pitch, inside and out."

"So now I'm supposed to be some kind of a carpenter?" Noah asked. "This doesn't mean that I am going to have to join a union, does it?"

"You are what I tell you to be," God said. "Either that or you'd better get to practicing your dog paddling technique."

Noah knew when he was beat.

"This is how I want you to do it," God said. "I want the ark to be a full three hundred cubits long and fifty cubits wide and thirty cubits high. I want you to make a roof for it – leaving below the roof an opening that is one cubit high and square all around. Put a lower, middle and an upper deck in it – and make sure you remember to put a big old door in the side of that ark."

"Why do I have to do all that for?" Noah asked.

"Because if you don't put a door in the side of the ark how are you supposed to get into it?" God replied. "Let alone out?"

"That's not what I was asking," Noah said. "What I was asking was why do I need to build this ark in the first place?"

"Because I am going to make it rain for forty days and forty nights," God said. "I am going to raise up the headwaters and flood all of the flood banks and I am going to wash this planet clean of sin."

"Well that's one way to do it," Noah said. "Wouldn't a broom and a dust pan be a whole lot easier?"

"I'm calling a flood down," God reiterated. "And you are going to have to be good and ready when I do."

"You figure I can do this all by myself?" Noah asked.

"You've got sons, don't you?" God asked. "And grandsons too?"

"We've even got some women folk," Noah admitted. "Although I can't rightly tell you what their names are."

"That settles it," God said. "Build me that ark and build it with a whole lot room inside of it – on account of I want you to bring into that ark two of all living creatures - male and female - to keep them alive with you."

"That's an awful lot of animals," Noah said. "Do I look like a zookeeper to you?"

"Not just animals," God replied. "I want you to bring two of every kind of bird, of every kind of insect and reptile and of every kind of creature that moves along the ground will come to you to be kept alive."

"So what will we feed them?" Noah asked.

"Take along every kind of food that is to be eaten and store it away as food for you and for them."

"We might need us some shovels," Noah suggested. "A few grocery carts, too."

"A few brooms wouldn't hurt none either," God added. "And maybe even a couple of industrial-strength dust pans."

"True, that." Noah reluctantly agreed.

"So do you have all of that clear in your mind?" God asked.

"Pretty near," Noah said. "I've just got one single question for you."

"Go ahead and ask it then," God said. "We ain't got all night."

"Just how big is a cubit, anyway?" Noah asked.

Chapter Ten – Building an Ark

ONCE HE'D GOT THAT WHOLE CUBIT THING straight in his mind Noah set out to build that ark.

Now – you can't just go ahead and build a 450,000 cubic cubit ark on top of the highest handy hill without some folks taking notice of your effort.

Around about the 75,000 cubic cubit mark Noah's ark began to attract a little unwanted attention from the more-curious of the local folk.

"Are you building a barn?" some of them asked. "Is that it?"

"No, I ain't building a barn," Noah replied.

"Old Noah has finally flipped his wig," others whispered. "It's senility or outright craziness. Stand back, it might be contagious."

What can I tell you?

A rumor is nothing more than a big mouthed lie flying on the wings of stupidity pretending to be truth.

"Father," Noah's sons said to him. "Everyone is laughing at us."

"Let them go ahead and laugh," Noah said. "Anyone who is trying to bring you down isn't worth worrying about on account of they are already standing at least three or four cubits below your notice."

"What's a cubit?" Ham asked.

"Shut up and keep building," Noah told him.

Then, after Noah finally broke down and told someone just exactly what he was building the situation got a whole lot worse.

"A boat?" the others laughed. "What good is a boat way out here? Wouldn't it have made better sense if you had built it down by the ocean?"

Noah put his head down and just kept on building.

"Maybe it's some sort of an artistic statement," another of the onlookers suggested. "Maybe old Noah has decided to become the world's first performance artist."

"Maybe he got some sort of creation grant from the government," another snidely added.

"Why don't you all go and begat yourself," Noah muttered into his beard.

Only the onlookers weren't the only ones who were actively talking behind Noah's back.

"My blisters are growing blisters," Shem complained. "And this here framing hammer is beginning to feel like some kind of a broken second arm to me."

"Just shut up and keep building," Noah repeated.

"Me and Ham and Shem are talking union," Japheth warned his daddy. "I'm fixing on running for shop steward."

"Shut up and keep on building," Noah said for the third time.

Even Noah's wife began to wonder.

"It's bad enough you can't remember my name," she said. "Now you get this whole crazy boat idea. Maybe you just need some sort of a hobby, honey. Didn't you ever think about bee keeping – or maybe even stamp collecting?"

Old Noah, he said nothing.

He just kept his head down and kept on building.

People came from far and wide just to stand around and watch this crazy old fool building himself a boat the size of Montana in the middle of an empty desert. Nearly every one of them had something hateful to say about it – but all of those insults just winged on past Noah's ears. He might as well have stuffed his ears with candle wax.

But every now and then some bystander would ask him the obvious question.

"Are you expecting some kind of a flood?"

And then – and ONLY then – would Noah look up and give that bystander a long flat-line look of you-just-hit-the-nail-on-the-head.

"Better keep your rubber boots standing close to the door," Noah would say to that accidentally brilliant bystander. "An umbrella and a rubber dinghy wouldn't hurt none, neither."

And then Noah would put his own head back down and get back to his ark building.

Let me tell you, God is one tough old foreman.

And he sure does frown on coffee breaks.

<u>Chapter Eleven – Saving The Worst For The Last</u>

IT'S JUST LIKE THE CARPENTER SAID - if you swing a hammer long enough, sooner or later the nail gets pounded down.

Noah and his family worked diligently at their craft.

No pun intended.

The time came when the ark was finally built.

"Slap a coat of paint on it boys," Noah said to his sons. "We're pretty near done."

"What color do we paint it, Daddy?" Ham asked.

"I think my hand has seized up on this hammer," Shem complained. "I'm not sure it knows how to let go any longer. I don't know if I can be trusted to swing a paintbrush."

"I think we ought to paint it pink," Japheth suggested. "Just the exact same color as cotton candy."

"We need to get us some groceries," Noah said to his wife.

"I'll make a list," she answered.

Then Noah filled the ark with every kind of food that you could imagine – and a few more that you might never have thought of – which got the neighbors wondering if old Noah hadn't set out to build himself the world's very first grocery store.

Then came the animals.

God sent two of every kind of animal possible to load up into that ark.

God sent aardvarks and African bush elephants. God sent buffalo and bandicoots and black widow spiders. He sent camels, and civets and Cavalier King Charles spaniels. He sent desert tortoise and dormouse and dragonflies. He sent earwigs and emu and emperor penguin; he sent field mice and flamingo and fruit bats. He sent giraffe and grasshoppers, hippopotamus and howler monkeys, ibis and iguana, jaguar and the dirty-mouthed jackal. He sent kingfishers and kangaroo, lions and lemurs and leopards too. He sent moose and marsh frog and monitor lizards, he sent nightingales and newts and Norfolk terriers. He sent orangutans and ocelots and octopi. He sent pigs and Pekinese and panthers and pugs. He sent quail and something else that begins with "q" and red-combed roosters and raccoons and a pair of snarling Rottweiler. He sent swans and snowshoe rabbits and some slow-moving sloth. He sent tigers and tawny owls and termites, too.

"Are you sure about those termites?" Noah asked God. "That ark IS made out of wood you realize?"

"Never interrupt me when I am busy begetting an alphabetic roll call," God told Noah. "Those termites will mind their p's and q's on account of I already told them to."

"Sorry I asked," Noah said.

"Never you mind being sorry," God replied. "You try and make it to zebra on your own and mind you – I want two of every kind of bird, of every kind of animal and of every kind of creature that moves along the ground," God told Noah.

"What if we get hungry?" Noah asked. "Them pigs is looking awfully pork choppish to me and my wife."

God had an answer to that question too.

"You work on keeping those two of every kind alive," God said. "That's your breeding stock. I'll send along some extras for eating."

Then God took another breath and sent Noah seven more seven pairs of every kind of clean animal, a male and its mate, and one pair of every kind of unclean animal, a male and its mate, and also seven pairs of every kind of bird, male and female, to keep their various kinds alive throughout the earth.

"That'll do a better job of keeping things going," God said – and Noah had to agree with him on that.

The very last animal to crawl on board Noah's ark was that big old snake.

"Look at that," Ham said. "Isn't that the prettiest little snake you ever did see?"

Noah took himself a look at that snake.

He had to admit that it was AWFULLY pretty looking.

"Do you think we ought to be letting that snake get on board?" Noah's wife asked. "What if he bites somebody?"

Noah thought about that.

"I can't see the harm in letting a little bitty old snake like that live on the ark," Noah decided. "He looks harmless enough to me."

"I think he looks cute," Shem said.

"We ought to paint him pink," Japheth said.

"I ought to get me a garden spade and black and blue him up some and heave him overboard," Noah's wife went on.

"Now don't be talking that way," Noah said. "That snake has got a right to live just the same as any of us does. After all, he is one of God's creatures too."

"I'm not so sure about that," Noah's wife said.

But the snake got on board the ark just the same.

<u>Chapter Twelve – Someone Left A Cake Out In The Rain</u>

AFTER ALL OF THE ANIMALS WERE SAFELY on board the ark the Lord God told Noah the rest of the details of his carefully thought out plan.

"In seven days from now I will send rain on the earth for forty days and forty nights, and I will wipe from the face of the earth every living creature I have made," God said.

"I still think a broom would be a whole lot quicker," Noah suggested.

"Whoever asked you?" God wondered aloud. "You can't even remember what your wife's name is."

So Noah went and told his family about what God had said.

"Seven days," Noah told them. "We've got to get busy getting ready."

"The ark is painted," Ham said.

"What color did you decide on?" Noah asked.

"We went with grey on grey," Shem said.

"How many shades of grey can you choose from?" Noah asked.

"At least fifty," Ham said. "The way I heard it."

"I still wanted pink," Japheth complained. "Like cotton candy."

"The next ark we build," Noah solemnly promised. "We'll paint it cotton candy pink. I swear to you."

That promise brightened Japheth up considerably.

"Do you think you can throw in a nail gun with that?" Shem asked. "I think I might be growing seriously allergic to hammers."

Noah's wife was upset for a different reason.

"Seven days?" she said.

"What's wrong now?" Noah asked. "Is there something that you've forgotten?"

"On the contrary," Noah's wife said. "There is something pretty important that YOU have forgotten."

"You're not going to bring up that whole argument about me forgetting your name, are you?" Noah asked, rolling his eyes so loudly that they rattled like Bingo balls. "I already explained on how I've got so much on my mind these days.

"No, smarty-pants, I'm not talking about my name," Noah's wife said. "I'm talking about your birthday. Seven days from today."

"Oops," Noah said. "I was never big on details."

Seven days later Noah's wife baked a three layer chocolate cream birthday cake and brought it out onto the upper deck to keep it safe from all of the animals.

Only nobody – not even Noah himself – got to taste so much as a bite of that three layer chocolate cream birthday cake.

Because – just like God had said – the sky opened up and it began to rain.

Do you know those soft summer rains?

Do you know those rains that spit and spat down lightly – like someone drumming his fingernails idly on top of a linoleum counter?

Do you know those calm and gentle kind of rains that whisper down and remind you of your mother's softest tear drop?

Well, this wasn't one of those kinds of rainfalls.

We are talking a regular frog-drowning gully-gurgling fence-lifting deluge – colder than polar bear pee and wetter than freshly clotted duck dung.

"We better close the door fast," Ham said. "She's coming up to be a real stump-drowning down-bucket thunder-pour."

"Not just yet," Noah said. "There's something that I am waiting to see."

Well sir, old Noah didn't have all that long to wait.

All of those folks who had been standing around and watching him work – laughing so hard that the tears ran down their toes – came running up to the ark and waving their arms in the air like they were trying to flag down a passing whooping crane.

"Let us in, Noah," the people called out. "We were wrong to doubt you."

Noah nodded grimly and then he looked up into the deluge, blinking away the raindrops as they fell.

"What do you say, God?" Noah asked.

God just reached down and closed the door shut on Noah – leaving all of those other folks out there in the rain to drown.

All that first night Noah and his family could hear the rain pounding down like nails being driven into corrugated tin.

"God created rain," Ham said.

"God created the flood of floods," Shem echoed.

"God created duck-drowning weather," Japheth said.

Noah closed his eyes – wishing he could close his ears to the sound of all of them sinful people going under.

"No sir," Noah said. "God has created a nightmare that man is never going to forget – or at least I'm certain sure that I'm not going to."

The rain kept on coming down.

And down.

And down.

Chapter Thirteen – How High Is The Water, Pappy?

THE RAIN CAME DOWN for forty days and forty nights and as the water increased the ark floated like a big fat-bellied solid cork duck.

It was just as God had said it would be.

Every living thing that moved on land had perished in the forty day flood.

"Maybe the birds lived through it," Ham said hopefully. "They could just rise up and fly out of this whole soggy rainstorm, couldn't they?"

"Don't kid yourself, son," Noah told Ham. "Rain this hard will bring a bird down to the earth – no matter HOW high he flies - and once he is grounded it will drown him colder than a fresh frozen frost-icle."

"What about the fish, Daddy?" Shem asked. "Couldn't the fish survive? I mean, it's not like they can drown is it?"

Noah thought about how he might want to boldly lie to his children right about then. Lying might have been merciful - only lying was a sin and lying to your children was even worse of a sin - and when you come to think of it too much sinning was exactly where the whole flood-the-earth mess first got started.

"No," Noah said truthfully. "You are exactly right. A fish CAN'T drown. But they can sure as heck suffocate if there isn't enough air in the water – and when it's raining this hard for as long as it has been there isn't enough air down there to raise up and cheek out a good-sized fart."

"You sure know an awful lot, Daddy," Ham said. "I bet you know everything there is to know about life."

Noah looked down at his feet.

"You listen to your Daddy," Noah's wife said. "The man is a regular know-it-all. You take out a handkerchief, Ham, and he'll happy to teach you how to blow your nose."

"I don't want to blow my nose," Ham said. "Right about now the boogers I've got lodged up there in my nostril-caves is about the only thing that I think is keeping me alive, breathing and sensible – what with the unwholesome stink that is seething out of all of those animals we've got locked up downstairs."

Ham was right.

The reeking funk from down below was thick enough that you could have sliced it up with a hunting knife and fried it for breakfast.

"Just try and breathe through your mouth," Noah wisely counseled. "It will be easier for you that way."

"I'm not sure which is worse," Ham said. "I breathe through my nose and I can smell it. I breathe through my mouth and I can taste it. One is as bad as the other come to think about it."

Noah didn't have much to add to that.

"Are you absolutely sure this is what God had in mind?" Noah's wife asked. "I mean maybe you just heard him wrong?"

Noah shook his head grimly.

"God said it," Noah asserted. "I don't expect he was talking through his hat."

"Does God wear a hat?" Ham asked.

"Only when it's sunny," Noah replied.

"Maybe what you say is so," Noah's wife said. "But I am beginning to wonder if God hasn't gone and forgotten about this whole family floating out here in the heart of this wide wet nothing."

Ham, Shem and Japheth nodded along with her.

"Never you mind what old what's-her-name has to say," Noah said, with a disgruntled snort. "What I am telling you is the honest truth. The only animals and fish and birds and insects alive are the ones that we are carrying in this here ark."

Ham and Shem thought on that a spell.

"I still think we should have painted the whole thing pink," Japheth added.

Chapter Fourteen – Two True Tales to Remember

IT TURNED OUT that God hadn't forgotten about Noah and his family and their lonesome ark – painted pink or not.

He was just taking his time, is all.

I'm not really sure what he was taking his time about but I have a couple of different theories to offer to you.

He MIGHT have been testing Noah's faith.

He MIGHT have been giving the water a chance to really soak in and clean the Earth up good and proper.

Or he MIGHT have been just taking himself a long old nap. After all, bringing down a deluge of that magnitude has got to be an awful lot of work for one fellow – even if he happens to be God his-own-self.

In fact I will bet you a hat full of silver dollars that God was just plain enjoying all of that sudden peace and quiet. I mean, you just think to yourself about all of those non-stop constant prayers that God has to listen to all day and night. It'd be a little like living in the complaint office of the universe – what with everyone and everyone's dog and everyone's dog's shadow praying for more money and straighter teeth and a set of washboard abs.

Even God needs a day-off sometimes.

You think about that the next time you get to praying for that winning lottery ticket to fall into your pocket.

So God went and slung himself a big old heavenly hammock hung between a pair of neighborly clouds and caught up on his "me-time" – like maybe about one hundred and fifty days worth. He had a couple of brew and a burger – but no cheese because even back then God was watching his cholesterol level – and he read a few chapters of the latest Stephen King novel.

Then he looked down at the Earth and he saw old Noah and his ark floating there in a sea of leaking doubt and he called down a calming wind to kind of blow on those floodwaters just a little and he encouraged those floodwaters to hurry up and drain themselves dry.

"You can ebb out now," God said to the water. "I've turned the floodgates off up here in heaven."

"It's about time," the floodwater replied. "My back teeth were seriously beginning to float. Would it have hurt you to install a Porta-Potty down here?"

So the water level went down just a little bit – just enough so that Noah and his family would notice and take heart.

Which happened around the very same time that the ark bumped into the mountain top.

"Ararat," Noah said.

"Gesundheit," Shem replied.

"We hit a rock," Ham shouted. "We're going to sink for certain sure."

"That's not a rock," Noah said. "That's a mountain."

"It looks like a rock to me," Shem said. "It's way too small to be a mountain."

"You're forgetting how high the water has got to," Noah pointed out. "That there rock is all that we can see of a mountain that is at least three miles high."

"How high is the water, Daddy?" Japheth asked.

"This isn't no time for singing, son," Noah replied. "Now you be quiet while I try and figure out just where we've got ourselves to."

"Well," Noah's wife said. "If you had thought to ask somebody for directions you might have found out that this was Mount Ararat."

"Gesundheit," Shem repeated.

"So who exactly did you ask for directions?" Noah asked.

"Well I thought about asking the old goat," Noah's wife answered. "But you were busy at the time – so I just read the road map."

"Have I ever told you just how much I truly hate it when you're being just a little bit too sensible?" Noah asked his wife.

That's two true tales as old as time being illustrated right there.

Number one true tale – love is all about putting up with each other's foolishment. Forget about all of those love songs and cupid arrows. He puts up with her, she puts up with him and both of them keep on grinning – well that's true love – as true as you can paint it.

Number two true tale – men will NEVER learn how to ask for directions.

Now which way was I going with this story?

Never mind.

I'll figure it out as I go.

Chapter Fifteen – The Difference Between Ravens and Doves

WHEN NOAH SAW that the waters of the world had shrunk down until that mountain that he was moored up alongside of had begun to look a little less like a simple rock in the water and a little more like the mountain that it was supposed to be he figured it was time that he took certain steps.

"I'm going to set loose a bird," Noah told his family. "The way that I see it that bird is going to most likely fly back and let me know if the water has dried up long enough for us to get out and light for a spell."

"So how long did you sit up at night dreaming up THAT feather-headed bird-brained idea?" Noah's wife asked.

"I love you too, honey-bunch," Noah said.

"What bird are you going to let loose, Daddy?" Ham asked.

"Well son, I am glad you asked me that," Noah said. "I have been thinking about letting loose the raven."

"Why did you choose the raven?" Shem asked.

"I figure he is smarter enough to know that he ought to come on back to the ark if he can't find any place that is dry enough to roost on," Noah explained. "I also figure he is big and mean enough to take care of himself just in case something else is out there. Him being dark means he can hide in the shadows if he has to."

Which made sense – as far as bird logic went.

So Noah opened up the upper window of the ark and he let that big old raven fly on out of that upper window – and it turned out that Noah was actually HALF right.

It turned out that raven WAS a whole lot smarter than most of the other birds combined.

He DID fly off just as far as he could fly – just like Noah planned it – but when he saw that there wasn't any land worth lighting on he flew back to the ark and settled on the tallest peak of the ark's roof.

He wouldn't come down no matter how hard Noah begged him.

"Is he supposed to be up there?" Ham asked Noah.

"Of course he is," Noah said. "That there is what sailors call a crow's nest – only on arks they call it a raven's nest."

Noah waited thirty more days and then he let a dove out the window.

Actually, he let two doves out – because the raven swooped down and caught that first one that Noah had freed.

"Dive, dove, dive!" Ham shouted.

"That dove is done for," Japheth said.

"What's that raven doing with that dove?" Shem asked.

"Why he's just showing that dove what a raven looks like from the inside out," Noah said. "Now let's let that second dove out through the window before that raven gets through giving that first dove the gullet's-eye tour."

The second dove flew out from the window of the ark and soared out just as far as he could fly before turning around and gliding back to the ark.

"I guess the water is still too deep out there," Noah said. "We'll just have to wait for a little bit longer."

Noah waited for seven more days before he tried releasing the dove again.

This time Noah was taking no chances.

"Son," he said to Ham. "You hold that chunk of rock in your hands and if you see that raven even looking sideways at this dove let him have it."

"Let the raven have the dove?" Ham asked.

"No, son," Noah said with a mournful sigh. "Let the raven have the rock."

Only I guess that old raven had enough dove to beak at for a while yet because he didn't stir a feather when Noah let the second dove fly free.

Noah stood there at the open window for two straight days.

"Do you think that dove is ever coming back?" Japheth asked him.

"Sure he will," Noah replied. "Unless he run into another raven – and that isn't all that likely, is it?"

Japheth wasn't that sure but he didn't want to let on that he wasn't certain – for fear of crushing his Daddy's spirits.

It turned out Noah was right after all.

On the third day that second dove came back and he was carrying a freshly-plucked olive branch in his beak.

"Hey Daddy," Shem said. "There must be an Olive Garden close by."

"That's good news," Noah said. "I was getting awfully hungry."

Then Noah waited seven more days and on that seventh day he went out to the upper window and he set that dove free and it flew off into the distant horizon and never returned.

"Well that settles that," Noah said. "I guess that it is pretty near time for us to leave this here old ark."

Chapter Sixteen – A Sky Full of Promise

ON THE FIRST MONTH of Noah's six hundred and first year on this Earth the water had dried up enough for him to feel safe in finally leaving the ark – which was a good thing because by now that ark had begun to stink worse than a dozen rain-soaked sheepdog rolled up in a cocoon of freshly-dropped elephant dung.

"Open all of the windows," Noah commanded. "Let the birds out first."

Ham and Shem and Japheth ran from one end of the ark to the other – opening up each of the windows.

The birds flew out like a great beating wave across the sky.

Noah watched as bark-feathered night jars and tiny beating hummingbirds and great wrinkle-necked vultures and huge-chested bustards and leggy sandhill cranes and elegant crested tinamou took off heavenward.

They were followed by Australian brush turkeys and dusky-legged guan and northern bobwhite and rock ptarmigan.

Bar headed geese and tundra swans and black-throated divers and sooty albatross.

Storm petrels and grebe and spoonbill and heron.

Cormorants and gyrfalcons, oyster catchers and blue-headed quail-doves.

There were birds with more names than you could shake a baptismal at.

There were birds with more colors than your eyes could ever register.

There were more kinds and shapes and colors of birds than you could list in a six foot tall stack of encyclopedia.

"Daddy, I have got a question for you," Ham said. "I am wondering just how come God decided to make so many kinds of birds?"

"You just answered your own question," Noah replied.

"Do you want to run that by me again?" Ham asked. "Your meaning seems to have eluded my way of thinking."

"You were wondering why," Noah patiently explained. "And that's your answer. God made so many shapes and colors and kinds of birds just so simple human beings like you and me might look up into the sky and wonder."

That made sense to Ham.

Of course he was tired at the time.

Then the insects crawled out and scuttled and buzzed and jumped from out of the belly of the ark.

There were mosquitoes and blowflies and damselflies and dancing flies waltzed like light-footed drunkards upon the vagrant wind.

There were long-nosed weevils and groaty-jawed cave crickets and armies of army ants and mechanical-looking assassin bugs and Texas long horned beetles and pale shrouded emperor gum moths and multi-legged millipedes and skittering book-gnawing silverfish and hookworms and locusts and sun burnt monarch butterflies.

"Why so many bugs?" Shem asked. "Most of them are nothing but nuisances, good for nothing but swatting."

"The insects do God's work as well, my son," Noah answered. "They are the janitors and the cleaning women of the planet. There is no fun in what they do. There is no glory in it either – but it is still about as important as you could care to think. Who else but a bug would crawl through the dirt and actually like it?"

That made sense to Shem as well.

"I'm hungry," Japheth said. "We ought to have a barbecue."

"First we let the rest of the animals free," Noah said. "Then we can talk about barbecue."

And that is exactly what Noah and his family did.

They sent all of the remaining animals and they kept a few back and they made a blood sacrifice to God – just the same as Abel did way back in Eden – and God smelled the good smell of those pork chops and lamb chops sizzling and the fire and he looked down and he ate his fill.

"You did a good job, Noah," God said. "And you're a pretty good cook, as well. Maybe not as good as Abel – but good just the same."

"I'm still alive," Noah pointed out. "Which is a lot more than Abel can say for his self. That's got to count for something, doesn't it?

God agreed grudgingly.

"Maybe so," Noah's wife added. "But I'm still the one who is most likely going to wind up cleaning up the kitchen after him."

"So what next, God?" Noah asked. "What do we need to do?"

"Well now it is time for you and your wife and your sons and THEIR wives to go forth and multiply," God said.

"Multiply?" Ham complained. "I hate mathematics."

"He's talking about begetting," Shem explained. "He's not talking about any kind of arithmetic."

"You folks need to get busy and fill this earth with ALL kinds of new people," God said.

"And will these people be any better than the last batch?" Noah asked. "Will these people will be free of sin?"

"Heck no," God told Noah. "People are people; no matter what color their skin might happen to be or what creed or religion they happen to believe in. People are fallible and they will get into trouble and they will do the wrong things just as nearly often as they do the right."

Noah chewed that over.

"So what was the point, God?" Noah asked. "What was the REASON for all of that rain and you drowning all of those people like you did?"

"I think I know the reason," Noah's wife said. "I think you're trying to show the world that EVERYONE can get a second chance and can start all over – no matter how much wrong they have gone and done. We all get a chance to a do-over in this life – and we ought not to waste it. We all get an opportunity to learn from what we did wrong in the past."

God smiled at that.

"You see, Noah," God said. "That's why I created women – on account of women are smarter than most of us men."

"Women know how to listen," Noah's wife said. "And I still haven't heard any of you using my proper name in this entire conversation."

"Your point being?" Noah asked.

"My point being WHY in this entire story didn't God ever think to write down my actual name?" Noah's wife asked. "Or to keep track of any of our son's wives or daughters? When you sat down and wrote the whole Holy Bible – why wasn't there room for our names? Do you have an answer for that, old man?"

She was angry and God couldn't blame her much.

God smiled at that too.

"I didn't write the Bible," God said. "It was men that mostly sat down and wrote it – and that was after they had heard the old stories being told to them time after time. It was men that forgot to write your name down. They were way too busy thinking about you as their wife or their daughters or the reason why they got up out of bed in the morning and smiled at the sunshine coming in through the window."

"That's a good story," Noah's wife said. "So what IS my name?"

"Your name is..." God began to say.

"I'm not asking you," Noah's wife interrupted. "I am asking HIM!"

She pointed right directly square at Noah his own self.

"Dear?" Noah stammered. "Honey? Sweetheart? Lovie-dovie? Doll?"

"You call me doll again," Noah's wife said. "And I'll black your eye so hard that Cain will come down with a serious case of Cain-mark-envy."

"Yes dear," Noah said.

"My name – in case you were wondering – is Emzara – if you read the Book of Jubilees or if you even bother talking to Saint Hippolytus. My name is Naamah, if you talk to a rabbi. My name is Dalilah if you ask an Anglo-Saxon. It is Norea, if you talking to a Gnostic and it is Vesta if you talk to a Cabalist."

"Now how am I going to remember ALL of those names?" Noah asked.

"Because YOUR name will be M-U-D if you don't learn how to remember," Noah's wife said. "Do you understand me mister?"

Noah looked down at the wet dirt at his feet.

"Yes dear," he whispered.

"I wouldn't exactly suggest forgetting her birthday, either," God added. "Let alone your anniversary date."

"And you – Mister High and Mighty God Over All – why don't you try explaining to me just WHY we should ever trust you again after you've gone and soaked out the entire population of this planet? Why in the world should we believe in you if there's the slightest chance that somewhere down the road you are going to lose your temper and throw another tantrum and flood us all out of house and home again?"

God thought on that.

"That's an awfully good question," God finally replied. "And I believe I have got a pretty good answer for you."

"I'm listening," Noah's wife said.

"Anytime I have something to remember," God said. "I always find that tying a string around my finger helps me to remember what it was I was trying so hard not to forget."

"I tried that once," Noah said. "And I just wound up trying to remember just HOW that string got tied around my finger and then it turned green and that didn't help one bit at all, either."

"I wasn't talking about you," God said. "I am talking about a promise. I am talking about a promise that is going to be my gift to YOU."

And when God said YOU he was pointing directly at Noah's wife – but he was thinking about all of us people who have grown up on this planet and have ever sat in the dark and wondered just what came next.

"Go on," Noah's wife said.

"I am talking about a gift – and whenever you give a gift you ought to tie a ribbon and a bow around that gift before you give it. So from now on – whenever it rains down hard enough I will tie a ribbon and a bow around the end of that rainstorm to remind me not to lose my temper one more time."

"Is that all of you've got?" Mrs. Noah asked.

"That's the best I can offer," God replied.

And that is exactly what God did.

He stretched out that rainbow right across the roof of the heavens at the end of every long, hard rainstorm.

Then God squeezed out a drop of every paint tube in heaven and he smeared those colors across that rainbow.

"Look at all those colors," Ham said. "Have you ever seen the like?"

"I have never seen so many colors in my whole entire life," Noah admitted. "It's definitely something to remember."

"Look Daddy," Japheth said. "I can see pink – like cotton candy."

And sure enough there it was – just as pink as certain newborn babies.

"Now let's get to the begetting," Shem said.

And so it happened – way back then.

Chapter Seventeen – Back to the Future

"I STILL DON'T GET all of that begetting business," I said to my Uncle Bob.

"Why don't you go and ask your Momma about that," Uncle Bob said. "On second thought, why don't you ask your Daddy? On third thought why don't you just forget about asking ANYBODY who might actually bear witness against me and go and look it up on Google, like I told you in the first place."

"I can do that," I said to Uncle Bob.

"So did that help?" Uncle Bob asked. "Do you see the reason why a fellow might actually want to stick around a little in Sunday School and listen to a few more Bible stories?"

I sort of half-nodded and half-shook my head like I was afraid to commit to an answer one way or another.

"I still haven't convinced you, have I?" Uncle Bob asked.

I shrugged sheepishly.

"I don't know what to tell you," I said. "When you tell the stories to me it makes perfect sense but when my Sunday School teacher starts flapping his lungs it all gets to sounding like so much babble to my ears."

Uncle Bob smiled at that.

"Let me tell you about Babel," Uncle Bob began.

IF YOU ENJOYED THIS FIRST COLLECTION KEEP AN EYE OUT FOR MY SECOND COLLECTION OF BIBLE STORIES – *UNCLE BOB'S RED FLANNEL BIBLE CAMP – FROM BABEL TO THE BULLRUSHES*.

Afterword

This new series of Bible stories is going to confuse the heck out of diehard Steve Vernon fans.

Let's face it.

As some of you readers might know I USUALLY write horror fiction and ghost story tales. I am far more comfortable writing about werewolves and vampires and ghosts and the like.

I am not even what you might call a church-going fellow. The sad truth is I have worked oddball shifts for all of my life – and as often as not I have to work most Sundays.

So why Bible stories?

At the heart of it I am a storyteller and I have ALWAYS enjoyed the stories in the Bible. It is just that so many of them are told in a style that tends to make it unpalatable for the modern reader – so I am just trying to spread the good word and tell a few good stories as best as I can.

I am NOT trying to convert anyone.

I am NOT trying to be particularly blasphemous. I believe God has a pretty good sense of humor and I like to believe that he or she would not be all that offended by the slightly tongue-in-cheek approach I have used to tell my tales.

Just stop and think about it for a moment.

How many of you folks have ACTUALLY sat down and read Winston Churchill's six volume history of the Second World War?

Hands up now – all three of you.

Now – how many of you folks have ACTUALLY sat down and WATCHED Saving Private Ryan?

There you go.

All that I am trying to do with these stories is to make the Bible just a little bit more accessible to a more relaxed kind of reader.

I hope that you enjoyed the read.

ABOUT THE AUTHOR

Steve Vernon is a storyteller. The man was born with a campfire burning at his feet. The word "boring" does not exist in this man's vocabulary - unless he's maybe talking about termites or ice augers.

That's all that Steve Vernon will say about himself – on account of Steve Vernon abso-freaking HATES talking about himself in the third person.

But I'll tell you what.

If you LIKED the book that you just read drop me a Tweet on Twitter – @StephenVernon - and yes, old farts like me ACTUALLY do know how to twitter – and let me know how you liked the book – and I'd be truly grateful.

If you feel strongly enough to write a review, that's fine too. Reviews are ALWAYS appreciated – but I know that not all of you folks are into writing big long funky old reviews – so just shout the book out just any way that you can – because I can use ALL the help I can get.

ALSO AVAILABLE

My Regional Books – from Nimbus Publishing

Haunted Harbours: Ghost Stories from Old Nova Scotia

Wicked Woods: Ghost Stories from Old New Brunswick

Halifax Haunts: Exploring the City's Spookiest Spaces

Maritime Monsters: A Field Guide

The Lunenburg Werewolf and Other Stories of the Supernatural

Sinking Deeper OR My Questionable (Possibly Heroic) Decision to Invent a Sea Monster

Maritime Murder: Deadly Crimes From the Buried Past

My E-Books

Flash Virus
Fighting Words
Tatterdemon
Devil Tree
Gypsy Blood
The Weird Ones
Two Fisted Nasty
Nothing to Lose –Adventures of Captain Nothing, Volume 1
Nothing Down – Adventures of Captain Nothing, Volume 2
Roadside Ghosts
Long Horn, Big Shaggy

FINAL DEDICATION

As Always I Dedicate This Book To My Wife Belinda

The guiding star this tale-telling gypsy steers his heart by.

Steve Vernon

www.ingramcontent.com/pod-product-compliance
Lightning Source LLC
Chambersburg PA
CBHW020510030426
42337CB00011B/315